COVENANT • BIBLE • STUDIES

Country Seer, City Prophet
The Unpopular Messages
of Micah and Isaiah

Robert W. Neff
Frank Ramirez

faithQuest® ♦ Brethren Press®

Contents

Foreword

The Covenant Bible Studies series provides *relational Bible studies* for people who want to study the Bible in small groups rather than alone.

Relational Bible study differs from other types of study. Relational Bible study is anchored in the story of God's covenant with the people of the Old Testament, the new covenant in Jesus Christ, and the covenant community that is the church today. This style of Bible study is for small groups of people who can meet face-to-face on a regular basis and covenant to support one another and grow together in an intimate group.

Relational Bible study takes seriously a corporate faith, a faith that relies on the contributions of all members. As each person contributes to study, prayer, and work, the group becomes the real body of Christ alive in the world. Each one's contribution is needed and important. "For just as the body is one and has many members, and all the members of the body, though many, are one body, so it is with Christ. . . . Now you are the body of Christ and individually members of it" (1 Cor. 12:12, 17).

Relational Bible study helps both individuals and the group to claim the promise of the Spirit and the working of the Spirit. As one person testified, "In our commitment to one another and in our sharing, something happened. . . . We were woven together in love by the Master Weaver. It is something that can happen only when two or three or seven are gathered in God's name and we understand the promise of God's presence in our lives."

In the small group environment, members aid one another in seeking to become

- Biblically informed so as to better understand the revelation of God;
- Globally aware of the interconnectedness of God's world;
- Relationally sensitive to God, self, and others.

Groups that use this study can build up the body of Christ and deepen faith by

- gathering as a small group of learners, open to God's word and committed to discerning its meaning;
- allowing the words, stories, and admonitions found in scripture to come alive for today, challenging and renewing us;
- thinking of all people as learners and all as leaders and appreciating the contributions of all;
- deeply respecting the courage and vulnerability of each person as he or she shares out of experience.

Each Sharing and Prayer section is intended for use in the hour preceding the Bible study to foster intimacy in the covenant group and relate personal sharing to the Bible study topic, preparing one another to go out again in all directions as people of faith in the world.

Welcome to this study. As you search the scriptures, may you also search yourself. May God's voice and guidance and the love and encouragement of brothers and sisters in Christ challenge you to live more fully the abundant life God promises.

Preface

Although you may not have thought much about Micah and Isaiah, they figure prominently in our worship lives. We Christians begin every Advent season with references to Micah and Isaiah when we sing "O little town of Bethlehem" or listen to Handel's *Messiah*. A visit to the United Nations reveals a gift from the Soviet Union—a sculpture of a man beating a sword into a plowshare, embodying the vision of peace in Isaiah 2:4 and Micah 4:3. Micah 6:8 embodies our vision for the ethical life: "What does the LORD require of you but to do justice, and to love kindness, and to walk humbly with your God?" In the Song of the Vineyard, Isaiah says that God expects from his beloved two things, justice and righteousness (Isa. 5:7), the essence of the ethical life. How shall we understand these two prophets who figure so prominently in our Christian tradition and in our ethical ideals?

Micah and Isaiah in the Context of the Eighth Century
First of all, we must locate these two prophets in the context of the eighth century before Christ. This period saw a huge upheaval in the political terrain of the ancient Near Eastern world, from the Tigris and Euphrates to the Nile. At the beginning of the eighth century, Israel in the north and Judah in the south enjoyed prosperity and relative absence of warfare—until the deaths of Jereboam II in 746 and Uzziah in 742. The first half of the century was marked by prosperity and peace in both Israel and Judah. Stable governments provided continuity of power and direction.

By mid-century, however, Assyria was beginning to consolidate its power in the north. Tiglath-pileser III, who began his reign in 745, led Assyria to follow a relentless path to the south, devouring any nation that stood in his way. Within thirty years (by 722) Samaria, the capital of Israel, had been destroyed. While Jerusalem survived destruction, Judea lost forty-six walled towns and fortresses to the Assyrian king, Sennacherib, who gave them to Judah's mortal enemy, Philistia, in 701. In a graphic report, this king says that he locked up Judah's King Hezekiah like "a bird in a cage" (Pritchard 246). From this invasion alone, it is suggested that 250,000 people were displaced. Cities became overcrowded with people seeking refuge. Whole families were separated from friends and relatives and carted off to new lands. Actually, nothing stood in Assyria's path until Babylon came to power with the defeat of Nineveh in 614. It was a time of war, distress, and suffering that lasted almost one hundred years.

Secondly, there was displacement of another kind—the economic oppression of poor farmers and laborers who had to give up land or go into debt to maintain an existence. The American archaeologist William Foxwell Albright observed through the excavation of ancient sites that during this time the development of huge and luxurious villas brought with it a decline in the quality of other types of housing (239). This stratification of society stood in marked contrast to the more equitable distribution of wealth in the prior two centuries of Israel's and Judah's life. Such development is referred to in the words of Isaiah: "Ah, you who join house to house, who add field to field, until there is room for no one but you" (Isa. 5:8). Micah observes a similar pattern: "They covet fields, and seize them; houses, and take them away; they oppress householder and house, people and their inheritance" (Mic. 2:2). These texts refer to land-grabbing by wealthy landowners at the expense of the poor and the destitute.

Thirdly, the eighth-century prophets understood that God had a history with the people. These prophets stood within the covenant tradition of ancient Israel. They were not inventors of a new morality, but representative of an old morality that went back to the Ten Commandments and the various codes of law intended to guide first the clan and later the society of the nation-state. When these prophets talked about land-grabs, faulty weights, and the oppression of widows and orphans, they could point to the standards of the law. Thus, the quotation from Micah 6:8, cited in the opening paragraph of this preface, is preceded by these words: "He has told you, O mortal, what is good." It is clear that the prophet had in mind a tradition—the law that all Israelites should have known and recited as a part of their religious devotion. The indictments that both Micah and Isaiah raised reflected the role of the prophets in calling Israel and Judah to obey the laws of God that had been handed down from one generation to the next.

Fourthly, the words of the prophets of the eighth century were written down in order to preserve what they had said. We learn of Nathan, Elijah, Elisha, Micaiah ben Imla (prophets of the tenth and ninth centuries B.C.) and others through narratives recorded in the historical books of 1 and 2 Samuel and 1 and 2 Kings. On the other hand, Hosea, Amos, Isaiah, and Micah all had their words collected and preserved in book form. They are referred to as the writing prophets. The community felt that what they had to say should be preserved, much as the laws had been collected to provide guidance to the community. As these prophets preached and prophesied, their disciples treasured their words and preserved them by repeating them and eventually writing them down (see Jer. 36). Even though their prophetic words were directed to the community of the eighth century, later generations found meaning and direction in what they had to say.

What is most remarkable is that we in the community of faith find meaning in these words even today. The prophets speak with divine authority to our situation as well. While history does not necessarily repeat itself, lessons can be learned. These prophets and this slice of history have connections to our lives—and not just in the songs we sing during Advent or in the ethical admonitions that we hear with renewed vigor. But just as the generation of the eighth century heard the Word of God in their message, I believe we can hear it as well. In the hearing of this Voice, we will be transformed.

1

Who Speaks for God?
Micah 3:8-12

Personal Preparation

1. Read Isaiah 1–11 and all of Micah. Read with speed rather than focusing on each passage. Highlight passages that strike you or sound familiar. If you choose not to mark up your Bible, use self-stick notes or write down the references on a piece of paper.
2. If you keep a journal, write down your immediate impressions of these two selections. Otherwise use a piece of paper.
3. Check newspapers, magazines, and the Internet for information about an event of your choice. Clip or print out accounts of this event from two different sources and bring them to the group session.
4. Consult a Bible dictionary, introductory material from a commentary or study Bible, or other source of information on Isaiah and Micah.

Suggestions for Sharing and Prayer

1. Play Christmas music as group members arrive. "O come, all ye faithful," "O little town of Bethlehem," "Hark! the herald angels sing," "Lo, how a Rose e'er blooming," and the first part of *The Messiah* are all based in part on texts from Micah and Isaiah.

2. Continue with a time for sharing concerns, joys, and observations. State your hopes for the upcoming sessions. Pray for one another.

3. Read a version of the *City Mouse, Country Mouse* children's story.

4. The author writes that although Isaiah and Micah witnessed the same events and shared some of the same concerns, their viewpoints were shaped by their "city" and "country" perspectives. Recognizing that we come from different backgrounds, identify yourselves as "city" or "country." Make a list of what group members perceive as the five best and worst things about city and country. Relate your impressions of first visits to a strange city or a new countryside. What did you notice? How did you react? What were your feelings?

5. Talk about the clippings you brought from different sources about the same event. What are the viewpoints of the various sources? What difference does it make in their reporting? How does this relate, if at all, to the different ways events might be viewed in scripture?

6. Write out Micah 3:11 on a large sheet of newsprint. Invite group members to illustrate the passage and list the complaints made against the rulers. What complaints could be made against your nation? your church?

7. Close by singing one of the carols or songs you introduced at the opening.

Understanding

When I was one year old, my family moved to Williamsburg in central Pennsylvania. Williamsburg was a small mill town, and we lived close to the local church. After my father finished his degree at Juniata College, we moved to Pittsburgh so he could continue his education at Pittsburgh Theological Seminary. The city made a huge impression on me—steel mills, more traffic, large church, tough neighborhood. This move to the city was a huge contrast to the protective environment of the secluded colonial-era valley known as "The Cove." This contrast of city and small town has remained with me all my life.

In my later years, I moved from Chicago to Huntingdon, Pennsylvania. Again, the differences in outlook and environment were startling and sometimes upsetting. For example, consider how two different American cultures celebrate the weekend that follows Thanksgiving. In Chicago, the day after the holiday introduces intense weekend shopping sprees. In central Pennsylvania, nothing matters except preparations for the opening of deer-hunting season. The contrast at the early stages of my life has been repeated in the later stages, only in reverse order. Perhaps that is what led to writing about Micah, who represents a small town outlook, and Isaiah, who thinks from the perspective of a large city.

The Heritage of Micah and Isaiah
While Micah and Isaiah both prophesied during the latter half of the eighth century B.C., there is a huge difference in their social contexts. Isaiah comes from the city of Jerusalem. He meets with kings and members of the court. He knows how to engage King Ahaz in conversation. He visits the temple, which is where his deepest vision of God occurs (Isa. 6). Isaiah is a child of the city, and his words reflect the elegance of the Davidic court. The words of Isaiah are among the loftiest utterances in the Old Testament.

On the other hand, Micah comes from a small country town, Moresheth-Gath, which was probably intended for the defense of Jerusalem twenty-five miles to the northeast. He was closer, it appears, to those dispossessed farmers and villagers who lost land to wealthy land-grabbers who likely lived in Jerusalem. Micah compares his words of lament to the cry of jackals and ostriches in the wild (Mic. 1:8). His great vision is of a courtroom where the mountains and hills gather to hear the testimony against the transgressions of Israel by none other than the God of Israel (Mic. 6:1-8).

This contrast led to the title of this study, *Country Seer, City Prophet.* Even though they speak out of different social contexts and with different modes of speech, these two prophets are seized by a common reality: the one Lord of all life, in this period of great turbulence, speaks with clarity to his servants. This variation in the backgrounds of these two prophets affected how they understood the monarchy. Both prophets inherited a religious belief that the Judean throne was given as a permanent gift to the house of David and that the capital city was the site of God's election. However, when they foresaw the judgment that would fall on the house of David, Isaiah depended upon the exalted language of the court in Isaiah 9:1-7 and 11:1-9 and divine throne names of the king to talk about future leadership. Micah, on the other hand, recalled the early days of David, who was a simple shepherd in the little town of Bethlehem, as a way to talk about the future (Mic. 5:1-6).

They also spoke against those prophets who upheld the popular belief that Jerusalem was inviolable and the Davidic king invincible. Such an outlook led to boldness in political planning by the reigning kings. In some instances, leaders exhibited a blatant disregard for political realities. Even more, this outlook led to a dependence on military might and political alliances that ran counter to the covenant promises of God. For Micah and Isaiah, the judgment of God was real, and accountability and responsibility were essential parts of their prophetic proclamation. These prophets challenged the political climate of their day.

A Fearless Prophet

Micah is fearless. In chapter 3 he proclaims that "Zion shall be plowed as a field; Jerusalem shall become a heap of ruins" (v. 12). His words are remembered for over a hundred years. When Jeremiah (ca. 600 B.C.) is threatened with death for suggesting a similar view, these words from Micah are quoted in his defense (Jer. 26). The reader can imagine what the citizens might claim. Micah would be portrayed as a traitor, a hireling of the Assyrian forces. The patriot, perhaps even a loyal servant of God, would believe that such words were unpatriotic and should not be uttered in time of war. The more I read these prophets of the eighth century, the more I believe they were grasped by God in a special way. They were inspired to do what they felt called to do, regardless of the circumstances and the consequences.

They could not have spoken with such authority unless they were grasped by a power greater than themselves.

This view is exactly what Micah claims: "But as for me, I am filled with power, with the spirit of the LORD, and with justice and might, to declare to Jacob his transgression and to Israel his sin" (3:8). In his claiming the gifts of power and might, we discover the origin of his fearlessness. These are the gifts of a warrior, but he is girding himself with the power of the Word rather than the might of a sword. With conviction, he speaks for God while the rest of his contemporaries have lost touch with the divine source of their message: "The seers shall be disgraced, and the diviners put to shame; they shall all cover their lips, for there is no answer from God" (3:7). Only the spirit could ignite a messenger with this kind of courage and radical message.

In the end Micah condemns both Judah and Israel for their transgression and sin, that is, for rebellion and missing the mark in the societal context. The people have failed in the most fundamental dimensions of society—the call for justice and for defense of the poor and needy. Society has failed; for this reason both Judah and Israel stand under unavoidable judgment. Micah sees the future not in averting God's judgment, but in his ability to see an end without coming to the end.

In session 3 we will examine the call of Isaiah, who frames the issues in a slightly different way but with the same result. The prophets who speak for God in this century are those who declare a message of accountability and responsibility. These prophets see the radical nature of God and are fearless in declaring it in the face of those who say, "Such words are unpatriotic and will weaken the people in a time of trial and war." In the next session, we will examine a group of people who were for hire and who wanted to appease their listeners by telling them what they wanted to hear.

Discussion and Action

1. As a group, answer the question, Who are these guys? Talk about your impressions of Isaiah and Micah. With which prophet do you think you would feel more at home?

2. Read Micah 3:8-12 aloud. Summarize the scripture in your own words. Would you feel comfortable directing this passage to leaders in your society? How would you phrase the message if you felt it was appropriate?

3. One of the accusations against Micah, according to the author, was that his statements (such as 3:12) were considered treasonous by his fellow citizens. What are the limits of criticism a country should allow? Should there be any limits? Why are some rulers quick to condemn criticism? How do you feel when you are criticized? What is the proper way to criticize?

4. Both Isaiah and Micah address the basic inequities of society, including the fact that the rich seemed to be getting richer while the poor were getting poorer. What similarities, if any, do you see between the time of the two prophets and our own? In your discussion, include information you may have read in the book's introduction.

5. In Personal Preparation you were asked to read all of Micah and the first eleven chapters of Isaiah. What is the basic complaint against God's people in these prophecies? Do Isaiah and Micah seem to be talking about the same thing? Explain your answer.

6. Those whom Micah condemns make the statement: "Surely the LORD is with us! No harm shall come upon us" (3:11). These words sound like what any of us might say to invoke God's protection. Do you think God always protects people, or are there circumstances in which God does not protect us? Explain. To what sort of security do we cling in difficult circumstances?

7. Is it possible to include condemnation, encouragement, hope, and despair in the same message? Explain your response, using examples from scripture and life.

8. When have you had to deliver a difficult or even damning message to someone who did not want to hear it? When has such a message been delivered to you? Is it possible for us to easily recognize problems, or do we need to hear such messages in order to get the point? What role does denial play in how many people view the world?

2

Messengers for Hire
Micah 2:6-11; 3:1-8; Isaiah 1:10-16

Personal Preparation

1. Read the texts aloud to yourself, if possible with a harsh expression of voice. How does it feel to you to be delivering such harsh messages?
2. Check a Bible dictionary or commentary to understand the festivals and rituals that the prophets are condemning.
3. The author recalls a statement by a pastor who felt he could not preach the truth in his church without losing his job. What truth might make you an outcast if you uttered it aloud?
4. Make a few notes in your journal or on a piece of paper about comments by these prophets that you feel might apply to you. Pray for insight and humility.

Suggestions for Sharing and Prayer

1. Greet each other and share refreshments. As you begin, play the song "Alas, alas for you," from the musical *Godspell*.
2. Take turns reading the Isaiah and Micah texts aloud, using as much invective in your voice as possible. Then enter into a time of silence. Invite one member to read Psalm 19 aloud, with all members joining in unison on the final verse: "Let the words of my mouth and the meditation of my heart be acceptable to you, O LORD, my rock and my redeemer" (v. 14).

3. Sing the hymn "Here in this place." Focus on the final stanza. In what way does your worship life speak to the problems of today? Is this a hymn that Micah or Isaiah could have sung? Why or why not?
4. Micah and Isaiah use profoundly vivid images for the accusations hurled at those whom they consider unfaithful. Is there a place today for such harshness? When do you think such language might be appropriate? When is it inappropriate?
5. In 6:5, Micah speaks about the story of Balaam and Barak. Retell this story for those in the group who may not be familiar with it. Perhaps someone could work ahead of the session to condense this rather long passage into a shorter version. The exercise can be made more amusing and fun if a donkey puppet is used.
6. As a group, rewrite the central prophetic points in a kinder, gentler manner. Share your thoughts on whether this would be a better, or worse, way to deliver this sort of message. Does the way a message is delivered influence you to be more (or less) receptive to that leader's message? Explain.

Understanding

At the beginning of the Iraq war, I had a conversation with a pastor friend who served a congregation of one of the historic peace churches. He said, "Bob, you know, if I were to preach against this war now, I would lose my job. The sentiments in my congregation are running so high that I cannot preach what I feel God has called me to say in these circumstances." This pastor did not believe that he was for hire, but the attitude of the congregation was that the minister was to represent their point of view.

The opening words of Micah's oracle against the prophets declare that seers and diviners have been hired to say what they have been paid to say. Micah reports eloquently about "the prophets who lead my people astray, who cry 'Peace' when they have something to eat, but declare war against those who put nothing in their mouths" (3:5). The prophets to whom Micah alludes can be bought for a price and will tell the people what they want to hear.

Many ancient societies viewed the prophet as a powerful intercessor who could and should persuade the deity to change the outcome of events and personal ills. The gods of the ancient Near East were often portrayed with a right hand of blessing and a left hand outstretched to receive the gift of the worshiper. Unlike the ordinary worshiper, the prophet had an inside track to petition on behalf of the devotee for his or her desired outcome. The prophet had the capacity to change the minds of the gods, and therefore the outcome of events.

The most extended description of such a belief in the Old Testament is the story of Balaam found in Numbers 22–24, which dates to five hundred years before Micah and Isaiah. Balak, the king of the Moabites, was in deep dread of the Israelites. He sent for Balaam to curse them, offering him huge wages to do this: "So the elders of Moab . . . departed with the fees for divination in their hand" (Num. 22:7a). Balaam, after many efforts, was not able to succeed because the God of Israel is not for hire at any price. Even the most powerful diviner of the region could not change the outcome of God's destiny for his people. However, the story is indicative of the popular belief that the purpose of religion was to get God to do what one wanted, and the popular prophets embodied this belief.

The Popular Prophets
Many popular prophets also felt that God's election of Israel made this people invincible. After all, God had chosen them from all the families of the earth to be his people. In an encounter between Amos and Amaziah, Amos prophesies the end of the Northern Kingdom. The priest suggests that Amos has been hired by the South to condemn the North. Amos makes it clear that he is not for hire, but is under the Lord's command (Amos 7). Amos declares that God has forbidden him to pray for the salvation of Israel, and then he declares the end of Samaria and the Northern Kingdom.

The background of this passage is shaped by the belief that speaking in the king's sanctuary obligates the prophet to represent the royal house's point of view. In 1 Kings 22, there are groups of prophets who do the king's bidding; they are expected to see the outcome of the future on terms that meet the king's expectations. This prophetic outlook was fed by the view that God had selected Israel, and therefore the country could not be defeated in battle. There were any number of prophets in Micah and Isaiah's day who also held this point of view.

The second belief was encouraged by the setting of worship within the context of sacred feasts and a sacrificial system. Isaiah blasts this view in one of his more elegant tirades: "I have had enough of burnt offerings of rams and the fat of fed beasts; I do not delight in the blood of bulls, or of lambs, or of goats. . . . Trample my courts no more; bringing offerings is futile; incense is an abomination to me. . . . I cannot endure solemn assemblies with iniquity" (Isa. 1:11-15, selected phrases).

In this passage, Isaiah says that real worship relies less on doing things exactly right on the altar, and more on developing right relationship with God. It matters little what you offer in sacrifice when you come into the sanctuary with blood on your hands ("with iniquity").

The popular prophets dismissed the social obligation of the worshiper and magnified the role of the sacrificial system in creating a right relationship with God. Isaiah linked worship with the recitation of the covenant tradition that depended on a devotional relationship with God. Solemn assembly in the covenant tradition was to bring about a renewal of the human community—neighbor closer to neighbor, a community that sustains life and cares for the dispossessed. That obligation escaped the popular prophets.

Prophets Out of Touch

While the messengers for hire were in touch with their constituency, they were out of touch with the other side of the equation, the God of Israel. The prophet "is the mediator between heaven and earth, messenger of God and intercessor in one"

(Buber 165). The problem with the popular prophets was that they were unwilling to hear the divine word. In fact, because of their orientation as intercessor alone, they were out of touch with God. "The sun shall go down upon the prophets, and the day shall be black over them; the seers shall be disgraced, and the diviners put to shame . . . for there is no answer from God" (Mic. 3:6b-7). By being tied to the constituents they served, they became blind to the source of their calling. They received no answers from God, but that did not stop them from speaking.

Micah recounts a long list of grievances against the behavior of Judah (Mic. 2:1-5). As he finishes this brief oracle, he quotes popular sentiment about not preaching on such things (v. 6). For the popular prophets, the moral life is separated from the confession of faith. According to Micah, "If someone were to go about uttering empty falsehoods, saying, 'I will preach to you of wine and strong drink,' such a one would be the preacher for this people" (v. 11). I don't believe that the prophet is saying that these prophets actually encouraged carousing. What he means is this: devotional life must issue in substance. These popular prophets smoothed over the call to obedience and focused on cultic sacrifice and the externals of ritual (6:6ff.). Micah points to a shallow religious life that believes God can be for hire and does not require anything in return. One might call this the commercialization of faith.

We will discover a similar dynamic in the next session. Even though Isaiah is overwhelmed by the awesome presence of God, the dialogical relationship between God and prophet remains. In it the prophet discovers that the people whom he is to represent are beyond healing. Isaiah and Micah stand in sharp contrast to the popular prophets by the way in which God grasps them and shatters their capacity to pray on behalf of a sinful people.

Discussion and Action

1. Micah uses harsh images in the accusations hurled by God at those who oppress the poor. Do you think these images would repel, alarm, convert, or annoy those to whom they were directed? Why or why not?

2. How do you react to criticism of this nature? How would you have phrased the same concerns?
3. Isaiah 1:11 directly states that God does not desire the offerings that are made in the temple. Yet it is the Word of God as revealed through Moses that calls for these sacrifices. How do you explain the contradiction? Which of our actions, in worship and in life, do we believe are called for by God? How might they become abhorrent to God?
4. In the Isaiah passage, there is a strong prophecy against the way Israel worshiped. All of these ways came from their understanding of God's Word. What has gone wrong, do you think, with the heart of the people that God seems to reject the worship offered to God?
5. The author writes, "Devotional life must issue in substance." What is the substance of your worship life?
6. What parts of your worship life do you believe are pleasing to God? What parts of your worship life today, or of your worship life in the past, might God find unacceptable?
7. The author writes, "Many popular prophets also felt that God's election of Israel made this people invincible." Do you believe, or do you think other people believe, the same about their nation?
8. In the ancient world, the belief was common that a military defeat for the nation meant that their god had been defeated by another nation's god in the heavenly realms. Do you observe this same belief among people with whom you live? Offer examples to explain your response.
9. How would you react to a Micah or Isaiah who came to your church with these words? Which of these words do you feel ought to be delivered to your congregation or to the church at large?

3

The Lord's Throne and the Lord's Commission
Isaiah 6

Personal Preparation

1. Read Isaiah 6. This is one the most famous passages of scripture in the Bible. Close your eyes and visualize the scene as Isaiah describes it. What elements engage the five senses?

2. Consult a Bible dictionary, commentary, or study Bible for information on the root words for the angelic creatures, and what this suggests about their appearance and function. Try drawing pictures of angels based on these biblical descriptions.

3. Cut out pictures of angels from greeting cards, magazines, and other disposable items.

4. Take time to silently listen, rather than speak, a prayer. To what ministry do you believe God has called or is calling you? How have or will you respond?

Suggestions for Sharing and Prayer

1. Begin with a short hymn-sing. The hymns "Holy, holy, holy," "Here I am, Lord," and "Great is the Lord" are appropriate.

2. Read Isaiah 6 aloud. This passage takes place in the heavenly court. Invite sharing of impressions about this passage gained from personal study. Then invite various group members to share how they visualize the scene.

3. The passage is one that ought to inspire awe. What special places in the natural world fill you with awe? What circumstances in human society have evoked the same emotion?
4. The author writes that "the whole experience is earth-shattering, for the divine has entered the human sphere." Talk about experiences members of the group have had regarding the divine presence in the human condition. Have these experiences been shattering? comforting? awe-inspiring? How does one know that such an experience has taken place?
5. Make a collage using the pictures of angels you cut from magazines, greeting cards, and other sources, as well as your drawings of angels based on biblical descriptions. What is the difference, if any, between the Bible's angels and angels as they are depicted in popular culture? What reason can you give for any difference?
6. In the movie *The Blues Brothers*, the two heroes of the film excuse whatever they do by saying, "We're on a mission from God." How does the feeling that you've been commissioned by God change your outlook? How can the feeling of being on a mission from God be abused?
7. Pray earnestly for each other, that all might hear God and respond in ministry and mission. Close by singing again the hymn "Holy, holy, holy."

Understanding

Most of us are aware of how unsettling political transition can be. God calls Isaiah at the death of a great king, in the face of an external threat from the powerful Assyrians and political challenges from neighboring states.

In the beginning of the chapter, we learn of the death of King Uzziah, who had governed Judah with great success for over forty years. However, our attention is not directed to the next Davidic heir on the throne. With Isaiah, we see a cosmic throne and a ruler whose reign extends over the universe. An earthly temple cannot contain his majesty; the mere hem of his garment fills the Jerusalem sanctuary. God's domain is not limited by the Davidic king, Jerusalem, or Judah; God's domain and action extend to the world. What Assyria, Samaria, or, for that matter, any other nation does is at the Lord's direction. Isaiah, at a moment of crisis, discovers a universal God who has no other challengers.

The Throne of the Lord

When we think of heavenly hosts, our minds usually call up cuddly cherubs or angels dressed in white raiment. In this text, the seraphs are winged serpents, terrifying in their appearance. They threaten any onlooker and evoke fear and awe. In addition, they keep God from being seen, since no one can look on God and live. Such creatures are often associated with protection of a deity or temple. Here they serve to enshroud God in mystery, to indicate God's awesome presence.

They also proclaim God's divine nature as holy and full of glory. *Qadosh*, the Hebrew word for holy, demonstrates the complete otherness of God, the quality that strikes fear in the unbeliever and awe in the believer. *Kabod*, the Hebrew word for glory, connotes weightiness and presence, the observable work of God in the world. The whole earth bears testimony to the invisible presence of God. "The prophet, living at the time of Uzziah's death and actively worshiping in the Jerusalem temple, is suddenly ushered into God's presence and given to experience a wholly different dimension of reality" (Childs 55).

The whole experience is earth-shattering, for the divine has entered the human sphere. Shaking the thresholds and filling the house with smoke all indicate a transformation of the temple as the place of God's empowering presence. In this moment, Isaiah cries out in despair, "Woe is me! I am lost, for I am a man of unclean lips, and I live among a people of unclean lips; yet my eyes have seen the King" (6:5). The encounter brings an awareness of his own sinful state, a state that is shared with his neighbors and friends. He shudders at his own uncleanness and is aware that he deserves death as he stands in the presence of the Almighty.

At this juncture one of the seraphim takes a coal from the altar, touches Isaiah's lips, and states that his "guilt has departed" and his "sin is blotted out" (6:7). This action removes Isaiah's guilt and atones for his sin. "Isaiah, cleansed from sin and blessed against every expectation, can now hear the voice of

God and answer it in the right way. . . . Only one who has rec-
ognized his sin and has been set free from it can do the will of
God" (Kaiser 81). In this brief scene, we find an example for the
rebirth of a sinner, who now in this cleansed state may receive
the Word of God. His new situation is an unmerited gift of God.

The Commission of Isaiah

The commissioning of Isaiah is quite different from the calls of
Jeremiah, Gideon, and Moses, who express doubt, inexperience,
and lack of ability. There is no hesitation here. When the question comes, "Whom shall I send, and who will go for us?" Isaiah
answers, "Here am I; send me." I remember my colleague at
Northern Baptist Seminary, Reidar Bjornard, with whom I joint-
ly taught an Old Testament class, doing a little dance, clapping
his hands, and saying, "Oh, I am so happy to do this task!" Of
course, this was a parody—an outlandish interpretation of the
prophet's response.

Dr. Bjornard knew the solemnity and weightiness of the situation. Such a circumstance does not bring glee, but evokes a
thoughtful and prayerful response. In fact, one may suggest that in
this moment of cleansing—in the wiping away of his guilt—the
prophet may have felt obligated to respond positively to the request
of the heavenly council. He had been changed by the encounter and
carried a responsibility in his newly pardoned state.

The dark side of this moment comes in the commission the
prophet receives: "Make the mind of this people dull, and stop
their ears, and shut their eyes, so that they may not look with
their eyes, and listen with their ears, and comprehend with their
minds, and turn and be healed" (6:10). We expect the prophet to
speak on behalf of the people so that they may change. We
expect the prophet to pray in such a way as to change God's
decree of judgment.

In Exodus 32:7ff., Moses cries out on behalf of people who
have sinned, and because of his intercession they are spared. No
such possibility exists for Isaiah. There have been many attempts
to soften this verse. Some interpreters say that it simply
describes the people's reaction to the prophet's message, which

was originally designed to bring the people to repentance. That's not what the text says. Isaiah brings a death sentence to a sick and sinful people who are beyond recovery in God's mind. Our normal expectation is that God is not punitive but redemptive, but that is not the case here. The implication is that by God's decree the divine history with Israel has come to an end.

A Horrified Response
The prophet is horrified. He is not by nature an enemy of his people. He cries desperately, "How long, O Lord?" Here we find the nature of all the prophets. They are all born with a love for their people. They are not jumping up and down to give a negative word and a hasty judgment. They are concerned for the survival of Israel. Yet God's answer is firm: "Until cities lie waste without inhabitant, and houses without people, and the land is utterly desolate; until the LORD sends everyone far away, and vast is the emptiness in the midst of the land" (6:11). Judgment is real; no one is spared. This outcome is like that of the wilderness generation, which was precluded from entering the Promised Land. The process is reversed here. Change cannot occur until the people are uprooted from a land that they have taken for granted.

Such change is reflected in the last verse. It appears that the stumps left standing in the field have been burned, underscoring the complete desolation of the land. However, the last fragment of the verse, "The holy seed is its stump," implies hope. Out of the ashes of the past order, a new future will emerge. Nonetheless, these verses seem to imply that no one escapes the judgment. In the next session, we will examine a court scene of another kind, one in the open country where God comes as judge of the people. Micah and Isaiah foresee a far different future for the people of God than the popular prophets, who sugarcoat what lies ahead and minimize the judgment of God.

Discussion and Action

1. What is Isaiah's mission? Does his mission in any way parallel your own experience with the church, or is it

totally different? Explain your response. How do you
respond when you are asked to help in mission and ministry? To what extent, even if the call comes from another person, do you feel it can come from God? How does
one tell?

2. The word *kabod*, the Hebrew word for weight, is also the
   word for glory. In his essay "The Weight of Glory," C. S.
   Lewis writes about how that weight and glory are
   reflected in every person. He suggests that we never
   meet mere mortals, but that we live in a society of
   immortals—and that this should affect the way we treat
   each other. Talk together about people you know who
   have real weight, depth, and substance. Is glory apparent
   in them? Is it hidden? Explain your answers as you share
   your stories.

3. Have you had an experience that you would consider on
   par with Isaiah's experience, or have you known someone who claims to have had such an experience? If so,
   relate the stories, and invite comments about how these
   experiences are like or unlike Isaiah's.

4. Try to identify the date of Isaiah's vision, based on the
   historical reference in the first verse of chapter 6.
   Discuss whether or not a time of political upheaval
   seems like a good time for a vision. When is there a
   good time for mission and ministry?

5. Isaiah describes a great deal about the heavenly court,
   but he does not describe God, other than a reference to
   "the hem of his robe." Is it possible to describe God?
   Why or why not? What descriptions have you heard?
   What have you said when trying to describe God?

6. Isaiah is told to "make the mind of this people dull, and
   stop their ears. . . ." Why wouldn't God want people to
   change? Is there an end to God's mercy? Explain your
   answers. What things in our time need to change? Are
   people today willing to hear messages about change? If
   not, why not? What does it take to be an agent of change?

4

The Lord's Court and the Lord's Attorney
Micah 6:1-8

Personal Preparation

1. Read Micah 6:1-8. Take time to carefully read the session text, especially with regard to insights about the way courtrooms operated in biblical times.
2. Compare and contrast the images in Micah with Isaiah's description of the throne room in the previous session. How does Isaiah experience the divine court? What is Micah's experience like? How do you think each prophet's experience is informed by his city or country background?
3. The author describes a court system quite different from what we experience in our own society. Read commentaries, the Bible, or search the Internet for other information on this court system.
4. The purpose of a court system is to provide justice. Take time to pray for justice in your life and in your community.

Suggestions for Sharing and Prayer

1. Sing "What does the Lord require" as you gather for prayer and worship.
2. The author writes about the court of the city gate. For some this might bring up images of old men in coffee shops dispensing justice. How far do you trust the sense

of ordinary people in your community, city, or country
to dispense justice?

3. Talk about your favorite courtroom dramas, movies,
or shows. Who are the main characters? How do they
function?

4. Discuss your experiences in court, positive and negative.
Who, in your opinion, stands up for the poor? Can you
name attorneys in your community who take the side of
the weak and powerless?

5. Play the courtroom scene from the movie *Cars*. Do you
think justice in the country is different than justice in the
city? If so, in what way?

6. Form two debate teams, acting as prosecuting and defend-
ing attorneys for the people in Micah's time. Present the
accusations, as well as a defense of the people involved.
Select one person to judge the presentations.

7. Identify ways in which individuals in both the group and
the community experience justice or lack of justice. Pray
specifically about the experiences people have observed.

8. Close by singing "Just as I am, without one plea."

Understanding

Sometimes in movies the difference between the city and the
country is best illustrated by the way courts are run. City courts
are places of great formality and dignity, where the rules are
observed in minute detail. Meanwhile, in the country, the judge,
the prosecutor, and the arresting officer are more informal folks
with an easy style and interchange. Nevertheless, they understand
the law. In both places justice is served, but the style is different.

In the last chapter, Isaiah came into the awe-inspiring court
of the Lord and saw God as a universal king. Micah builds on
this image and sees God as universal judge who comes to exe-
cute justice. Micah portrays the images in the heavenly court as
pastoral—mountains, hills, and earth. Micah opens with God
bringing judgment against Judah and Samaria, with the ominous
description of mountains melting and the valleys bursting open
like wax near a fire before the judgment of God (Mic. 1:3-4).

The Trial Scene

Micah 6 describes a trial scene involving various parties. The Hebrew legal system was more free-flowing than ours. In towns, courts assembled in the city gate, where accuser and accused exchanged charges and countercharges. Roles could be reversed at any time; accuser could become accused. The elders of the community stood by and eventually rendered judgment. In chapter 6, the courtroom is out in the open country. In place of elders in the city gate, here the mountains and hills are called to hear the trial. Chapter 6 uses the technical Hebrew term for trial, *rib*, four times in the first two verses. The noun and the verb forms are translated as "controversy," "plead a case," and "contend" in the NRSV.

God begins with an invitation for the people to present their case. God implies that they must have found something wrong with their Lord to behave in such a disobedient fashion (descriptions of the people's sins are found in the early chapters of Micah). God reminds the people to prepare a case so that their charges can be heard. This first invitation is met with silence.

Questions from God Without Answers from the People

The Lord continues with a question: "O my people, what have I done to you? In what have I wearied you? Answer me!" (v. 3). Again there is silence. God responds by outlining the history of salvation. This history begins with deliverance from bondage in Egypt, where the Israelites suffered under hard labor imposed by Pharaoh (see Exod. 2–15). God sent leaders like Moses, Aaron, and Miriam to guide them into freedom (see 6:4). The next scene describes an episode from Israel's wandering in the wilderness when King Balak of Moab tried to have them cursed by Balaam, who was prevented by God from doing this (see Num. 22–24). Shittim is on the east side of the Jordan, the last camp of Israel before entering the Promised Land. Gilgal was their first camp on the west side, after crossing the Jordan River (see Josh. 3–5). Verses 3 and 4 summarize the salvation history of the people of God. Longer testimonies can be found in Deuteronomy 6:20-25 and 26:5-9, as well as in Joshua 24.

There are two important Hebrew verbs in these verses, *zakar* (remember) and *yada'* (know). It is clear from passages like those in Deuteronomy that to remember is to internalize the past in such a way that all future generations would have the same experience as the first generation. The interpreter can sense this in Deuteronomy 26:5-6, where suddenly the speaker is in Egypt with his or her predecessors. When we declare our faith in Jesus Christ, we share the same faith experience as the first believers. That's what is implied in this text.

The verb *to know* carries with it intimate knowledge of someone, as in the relationships between husband and wife or among dear friends. To know someone brings an in-depth aware-ness of the other, a consciousness of the other's likes and dis-likes, concerns and joys. For the community of faith, to know and remember God's salvation is to be aware of a transformed life and relationship.

The People's Question
The people respond to God's recitation by asking a question that implies distance from God and a lack of understanding about what is required in this relationship: "With what shall I come before the Lord?" (Mic. 6:6). Such questions appear in the Psalter: "O LORD, . . . who may dwell on your holy hill?" (Ps. 15:1), and "Who shall ascend the hill of the LORD?" (Ps. 24:3). These questions are the context for worship. In some traditions these moments of self-examination come before the Eucharist or love feast.

The people are thinking in terms of the sacrificial system. The first level of sacrifice in this passage is a burnt offering of one-year-old calves. This commitment is great, since in burnt offerings the entire animal is consumed; the worshiper receives nothing back. In the second part of the response, multiple gifts are implied. "Thousands of rams and ten thousand rivers of oil" model the extreme extravagance of Solomon at the dedication of the temple (1 Kgs. 8:62ff.).

The third level of response resurrects a behavior that had been condemned in Israel—the sacrifice of a child, which in other cultures was viewed as the ultimate show of commitment to a deity.

The people might be thinking about the sacrificial system, but that is not what God is concerned with. In Micah 6:4-5, God recalls the covenant community; it is relationships within the community of faith, and not sacrifices, that concern God.

The Attorney's Answer
At this juncture in the text, the prophet steps forward as a prosecuting attorney. The people have declared that they are in a quandary about what to do. Micah states categorically that God has shown them what is required. They have had a five-hundred-year history with their Lord, and there has been a consistent message through all these years: "He has told you, O mortal, what is good" (6:6). Micah then summarizes Israelite law, much in the fashion that Jesus does before the rich young ruler in Matthew 19:16ff. The summary in verse 8 is often seen as the high point of the ethical life in the prophets.

There are three injunctions. The first, "to do justice," may imply giving true testimony in a trial situation, or maintaining property rights and true weights in the marketplace. Given the circumstances of this prophet and Isaiah, I would suggest it also means standing up for the rights of the dispossessed, the poor, the needy—like the widow and the orphan. The second, "to love kindness," follows the Greek *eleos* in translation. The Greek suggests an attitude of compassion and kindness. The Hebrew word *hesed* implies faithful loving, covenant devotion, avoiding changing commitments when life gets tough. The third, "to walk humbly with your God," suggests humility and lack of arrogance in the expression of one's faith. In wisdom literature, the word *humble* implies caution or modesty in one's daily walk. The essence of this summary of law is to seek justice for the lowly, maintain one's devotion to God and neighbor, and to walk with God in modesty (my version of the text).

Discussion and Action

1. Compare Micah 6 with Isaiah 6. In both cases the prophets speak from the perspective of being in God's court, but they give two different impressions. Name the differences and similarities.

2. What protections are offered to people on trial today in our country? When rights are denied to prisoners taken in the war on terror, what are the effects? How might God view these courts?

3. What has been your experience in real-life courts? Have you ever been called to jury duty, or participated as a judge or attorney? Have you ever been a plaintiff or defendant, or attended the trial of a relative or friend? How did people dress? Who was involved? What were the proceedings like? What was the outcome?

4. Invite people to reflect on whether or not the courtroom drama as described in Micah seems fair. In this courtroom, who speaks for God? Who speaks against God?

5. The author speaks about the Hebrew words for "remember" and "know." How are these words defined in the Hebrew? How does he say that this is related to our experience when we have faith in Jesus Christ? Is this how most people define these words and relationships? Explain your response.

6. Micah 6:8 is identified by the author as the attorney's answer. How are the three requirements defined in this book? How do they translate in our daily living? What specifically needs doing in our communities and nations for these to become a part of our daily living? What actions can you and your group perform in the community to guarantee justice, mercy, and a humble walk with God?

5

The Song of the Vineyard
Isaiah 5:1-7

Personal Preparation

1. Write out Isaiah 5:1-7 in longhand. Alongside your writing, create a series of drawings that illustrate the story.
2. Read Luke 13:6-9. As before, read by writing, and illustrate as you go along. Write two sentences that compare and contrast the action in the two passages. Bring your sentences and illustrations to the session.
3. The Isaiah passage begins as a love song, one that seems to end in disappointment. Look for an instrumental version of a favorite love song, jazz if available, that builds around the themes of the song without simply following the melody. Bring it to the session.
4. Return to the Isaiah passage. Try to envision yourself as the disappointed narrator, then as the person described as a garden, and finally as one of the "people of Judah" who is called to judge the situation. Which viewpoint more accurately reflects your experience?

Suggestions for Sharing and Prayer

1. As you gather, share grapes or grape juice and bread. Talk a little about what has happened during the past week.
2. Begin by playing the love songs brought by group members. Do not give the title of the song. Invite group members to call out the name of the song as soon as they recognize it.

3. Using the song titles or words from songs as you remember them, offer aloud sentence prayers of love and faithfulness to God. The leader may close with a longer prayer.
4. How comfortable are you with language such as "my beloved" to describe God's relationship with you? The author, Bob Neff, refers to the Song of Solomon and demonstrates that the images of bridegroom and bride are used for God and the people. Do you think of your relationship with God as one of lovers? Why or why not?
5. Share your illustrated versions of Isaiah 5:1-7 and Luke 13:6-9. Pass them around, and if possible post them on a bulletin board or wall. Reflect on your sentences, comparing and contrasting the actions in the two passages. Which best reflects your experience, both as one who has trusted others or as one who was trusted by others or by God?
6. Write a love letter to God. Consider ways that as a church, a nation, or as a group you may have fallen short of God's expectations. Write down ways in which you will make amends. Close with expressions of praise.
7. If there is time, brainstorm a list of ways the group might exercise faithfulness and discipleship in the coming year. Prioritize the items, and pray over the list. Close with a hymn.

Understanding

One of my professors at Yale Divinity School was B. Davie Napier, who taught Introduction to the Old Testament and Old Testament Theology. On the last day of class in my senior year, he sat down at the piano in a large lecture hall and began to play jazz as an assistant passed out test papers. For those of us who needed the course to graduate, this moment seemed like a mixed metaphor—entertainment in the context of a last judgment.

In Isaiah 5:1-7, the city prophet surprises the reader by using a country image: a vineyard. Granted, his is a romantic view of the country, but sometimes a person from outside sees more clearly. The prophet sees the whole history of Israel from the standpoint of this country metaphor.

This passage, written as a love ballad sung on behalf of a distant friend, catches us off guard. At that time, it was not uncommon for a bridegroom to send his best friend to communicate with his bride. This meant that the friend would carry a message from the bridegroom to the bride while they were separated from each other.

The song's introduction alludes to the bridegroom's love for his beloved (v. 1). This interpretation is underscored by the use of vineyard as a metaphor for "lover," as in the Song of Solomon (1:6; 2:3, 15; 4:12-16, etc.). The introduction and description of the setting are followed by three stanzas of the song (vv. 1b-2, 3-4, 5-6). An interpretation is given in verse 7 (Kaiser n.p.). Continuing on, the bridegroom and bride will be identified. The opening speaker is the prophet himself, who may have presented such a ballad in the context of a harvest festival.

The Vineyard
The first stanza (5:1b-2) notes that the beloved had a vineyard on a fertile hill. This vineyard was cared for in every way possible. The ground was cleared of stones and planted with the best vines. A protective tower was built to alert the keepers of the vineyard of danger, and a wine vat was built to process the harvest. With such precision and care, one would expect the very best grapes and the very best wine. However, the vineyard yielded a disappointing harvest of wild grapes.

What lies behind the song? In the earliest confessions in Israel's life, the worshiper recited that "[God] brought us into this place and gave us this land, a land flowing with milk and honey" (Deut. 26:9). When the spies were sent to scout out the Promised Land, they returned with a cluster of grapes so large that it had to be carried on a pole between two men (Num. 13:23). The land was perceived as a giant vineyard, laden with produce. Water purity in the city was an iffy thing. Wine with alcohol would kill bacteria and was a purer drink for the city dweller. Wine in this period was an important commodity and linked city dweller with the country.

Deep within the confessional life of Israel was the conviction that God gave them this land not because they deserved it, but because he chose (loved) this people. The land was fertile and had everything needed for their well-being. Such a gift called for stewardship and right relationships among all the citizens. It led to a belief that one could not gain advantage over another citizen. Laws were set in place to preserve this view of the land as a gift, such as the year of Jubilee (Lev. 25) or the sabbatical year (Exod. 23:10).

The Surprise

The first stanza of the song is a recitation of God's activity with the people, but an unfortunate event has happened. The vineyard has failed to produce appropriate fruit. The beloved had done everything that was required. Nonetheless, his cultivation and care has been rejected. It must be said at this point that the identity of the beloved has not been made known.

There is an abrupt change by the second stanza (vv. 3-4). The prophet is no longer speaking; now the beloved addresses the people directly. He asks the people to judge between him and his vineyard: "What more was there to do for my vineyard?" There is an awkward silence. This silence is followed by another question: "When I expected it to yield grapes, why did it yield wild grapes?" Again there is a long silence.

The listeners are not left hanging. The Beloved now answers in the absence of a response from the audience. Thistles and briars will cover the land. Worst of all, it will be plundered and laid waste. When the walls that protect it are torn down, enemies may overrun the vineyard and destroy it. At the very end, the owner of the vineyard is revealed in the words, "I will also command the clouds that they rain no rain upon it (v. 6b). The only Beloved who can do that is God.

What began as a song in harvest time ends with words of judgment. This is why I began with the story of B. Davie Napier and the mixed metaphor of jazz and the judgment of a test. However, this text is even more poignant, because the listeners, unlike the students who knew what was coming, had no idea that they were under judgment. They thought they had the never-ending protection of God and discover in a harvest celebration that they have been rejected. Not surprisingly, they were shocked by the unexpected turn of events.

The Real Speaker

The final verse (7) leaves no doubt about the players in this drama. The vineyard is identified as the house of Israel and the people of Judah. The Beloved is now proclaimed as the Lord of hosts. The audience now knows who the real speaker in the drama is. He is the Lord!

It is hard to find a play on words in English that mimics the concluding half line in Hebrew, but spelling may help. Justice in Hebrew is *mishpat*; and bloodshed is *mishpach*; and righteousness is *tsedeqah*; and iniquity, which may be a better translation for cry, is *tse'aqah*. Thus, the prophet concludes with the distinction of true grapes and wild grapes. A true harvest promotes justice and righteousness in the land, not bloodshed and iniquity. The task of the people of God is to maintain a community of right relationships where one group does not gain advantage over a less fortunate group.

The ballad of Isaiah reflects the history of God with his people and their deliverance into exile. In the New Testament, these verses are reflected in the parable of the wicked tenants (Matt. 21:33ff.). In a briefer version, the Gospel repeats the story of the vineyard, extended to include God's history with his people until the time of Christ.

In this version, the vineyard is given over to tenants because the landowner must go to a distant country. When the harvest time comes, his representatives are beaten, stoned, or killed. Then he sends his own son, who is killed because the tenants believe that with his death they will take control of the land for themselves.

In the parable, just as in Isaiah 5, there is a difficult question: "What will the owner do with these tenants?" This time the listeners give an answer: "These tenants will go to a miserable death" (v. 45). Clearly the conclusion of the parable underscores several of the teachings in Isaiah. The land is a gift; its produce, righteousness, is for the landowner, and those who are called into the vineyard are simply stewards of a divine calling. To reject God's gift and claim it as one's own without responsibility leads to death. On the other hand, appropriate stewardship brings life and well-being to all parties who dwell in the land.

Discussion and Action

1. What is the toughest test you have ever faced? Do not limit your answers to tests you may have taken in school. According to your reading of this session, what test did God's people face, and how did Isaiah feel about the way they met expectations?

2. Isaiah uses the image of a gardener and a garden. Compare the work involved in creating and maintaining a garden with God's work for us and with us. If you are not a gardener, what is another image that comes to mind?

3. The narrator of the Isaiah passage is identified by the author as "the Lord of hosts" and the garden is identified as "the house of Israel." How do you suppose the people who first heard this passage reacted? Did they see themselves as unfaithful? How do you think people in your country would feel if they were told that this parable referred to them? Would it be a fair comparison? How do we react to criticism of ourselves as individuals and as a nation?

4. In this book we see that both the country prophet and the city prophet use the images of growing and land and expect that we will understand how important it is to take care of the land. How do you, your group, and your church actively take part in the stewardship of the earth? Do you consider it an important part of your devotion and discipleship?

5. Isaiah talks about useless grapes. In your life experience, what endeavor has required great effort yet led to great disappointment? What results did you experience? Did you abandon further efforts or try harder? How might this relate to Isaiah's parable? What insights might such

experiences give us into the feelings of God as related by Isaiah?

6. The passage describes a great turnaround: from expressions of love to a disappointing harvest to words of judgment. What judgment or merit do you think our generation, our church, has earned?

7. The author references the parable of the Wicked Tenants in Matthew 21:33-46. What does the owner say he will do to the tenants in this parable from Jesus? Compare this to the words of Jesus about the fig tree that is not producing in Luke 13:6-9.

6

The Tragedy of Rural Life in the Book of Micah
Micah 1:8–2:5

Personal Preparation

1. Read Micah 1:8–2:5 aloud.
2. Look up Sennacherib in a Bible dictionary to gain a little more insight into this passage and this session.
3. Write down a list of key words from this passage. Pray about the words as if you were the one under judgment. Pray as if you were the one judging. Bring the list to the session.
4. There is terrible suffering in different places in the world, some of which might be preventable if proper help were given. Look up websites for the New Community Project, Heifer International, the Gates Foundation, or other sites to find statistics about disparities between developed, developing, and undeveloped nations. What solutions, if any, do these websites suggest?

Suggestions for Sharing and Prayer

1. Greet one another as you arrive, and share news of the previous week. Play "And he shall purify" from Handel's *Messiah*. Pray for each other and for concerns you may share.
2. Take a moment once again to identify yourself as a city person or a country person. Explain why you feel this way. Say a little about your life journey and where you

have lived over the course of your days. How does this
affect the way you view things?
3. Read Micah 1:8–2:5 aloud together. Share any insights
   you may have gained about Sennacherib and the situation facing God's people as described by Micah. What,
   if any, current situations seem similar to this?
4. Consider what you know about rural life, both in your
   country and abroad. What is the ideal picture people
   have about life in the countryside? What is rural life
   actually like? Share what you learned from websites
   about the problems facing people around the world.
   Have you and your group taken any steps to help others?
   What results, if any, do you think your work has had?
5. What are the obvious disparities in the ways people live
   in different places? How much of it is connected to
   being rural or living in the city? How much of it has to
   do with living in the developed world and living in the
   so-called Third World?
6. To some extent, it appears that Jerusalem has written off
   the country towns that have been vanquished. Are there
   groups in our own society who are written off? Who are
   they? What suffering is accepted by our society, and by
   the world?
7. Enter into a time of prayer for those who are impover-
   ished in Africa, Asia, and other parts of the developing
   world. Invite each person to pray for an individual,
   region, or nation. Issue a call for the Spirit's guidance as
   the group discerns ways to turn concern into action.

Understanding

The Book of Micah begins with God coming out of his holy
place to judge the earth. The mountains and the high places melt
at the awesome presence of God. The people of Israel and Judah
expect that Assyria will receive the rod of God's anger. But that
is not the case. Instead, judgment falls on the capital cities of
Israel and Judah, Samaria and Jerusalem. Samaria will become
nothing more than a heap of rubble and all her religious centers

will be destroyed (1:6-7). At about the middle point of Micah's prophetic ministry, in 722 B.C., Samaria is destroyed. This destruction serves as an example and warning for Judah and Jerusalem, to whom Micah now directs his attention.

In Micah 1:8-9, the prophet focuses his attention on Judah. Micah tells the people in the south to begin a season of mourning, because the disaster in the north has reached the gates of Jerusalem. Almost immediately, the prophet moves from Jerusalem to the countryside, to the towns and villages west of the capital city. Many of these towns are difficult to identify, but they lie in the hill country between Jerusalem and the Philistine city-states along the Mediterranean coast. They are Gath, Beth-leaphrah, Shaphir, Zaanan, Beth-ezel, Maroth, Lachish, Achzib, Mareshah, Adullam, and the prophet's hometown, Moresheth-gath. As a hometown boy, the prophet makes fun of some of these towns by using word plays on their names, much as we do today with athletic or economic rivals. For example, Lachish, a large and prestigious town, is mocked for depending upon horse-power—steeds hitched to chariots—instead of God's power. The Hebrew word for steeds is *larekesh* (1:13). Achzib, a town known for treachery, lives by deception (*'akzab* [the Hebrew word for lying, *kazab*], 1:14b). While the policies of Jerusalem are responsible for the invasion by the Assyrians, the small towns are the ones who take it on the chin.

Sennacherib's Devastation of the Small Towns

In 2 Kings 18:13, we read that Sennacherib invaded Judah from the west and captured many of the small towns in the hill country on his way up to Jerusalem. Sennacherib's own battle report corroborates this devastation: "As to Hezekiah, the Jew, he did not submit to my yoke. I laid siege to 46 of his strong cities, walled forts, and to countless small villages in their vicinity, and conquered them. . . . I drove out of them 200,150 people, young and old, male and female, horses, donkeys, mules, camels, big and small cattle. . . . Himself I made a prisoner in Jerusalem, his royal residence, like a bird in a cage" (Pritchard 288). Later in the report, Sennacherib relates that he gave all these captured cities and towns into the hands of the Philistine city-states. This last event is alluded to in Micah 1:16 when he says, "they have all gone . . . into exile."

Of these cities, Lachish was the most important and largest because it served as the key fort on the way to Jerusalem. Its job was to delay and stall enemy armies as they moved to the interior of Judah. From another era, the description of the ominous advance of foreign troops outside this walled city is described in letters unearthed by archaeologists: "And let my lord know that we are watching for the signals of Lachish, according to all indications, which my lord hath given, for we cannot see Azekah" (Pritchard 244). It appears from this letter that the smoke signals of key guard cities had disappeared, in a way announcing the advance of the enemy by their absence. Lachish was destroyed by Sennacherib, who left the Judean landscape in shambles and controlled by foreign powers.

As contemporary observers, we tend to think of war and terror in terms of capital cities like Berlin, Baghdad, Teheran, Washington, New York, London, or Madrid. This country seer points us to the rural devastation that is part of all war. In a recent description of the war in Iraq, Thomas Ricks, in his book *Fiasco*, describes the behavior of America's 4th Infantry Division in the town of Auja: "Kicking in doors, knocking down buildings, burning orchards, and firing artillery into civilian neighborhoods. . . ." Think of Darfur and the rural devastation of farming families and villages. Our picture of war follows the clash of armies and the destruction of large cities. Ask anyone in the rural South about the Civil War, and they will recall the devastation of farms and the loss of crops as if it were yesterday. Micah directs our attention to the rural areas where people and landscape are destroyed.

Land-grabbing and Covetousness

Micah 2:1-5 describes another kind of devastation: the loss of land by rural farmers to wealthy landowners. He expresses it this way, "They covet fields, and seize them; houses, and take them away; they oppress householder and house, people and their inheritance" (2:2). Whether these land-grabbers were Jerusalem nobles or local landlords who foreclosed on loans and gobbled up land from small farmers is debated (Hillers 33). Some suggest that they might have been government and military officials who inhabited these guard towns (Wolff 48). Limburg suggests that they may have been "the moderately well-to-do who wanted some property for . . . vacations in the country, with fresh air, a few horses, and a marvelous view" (169). The picture painted by the prophet is clear: the small farmer is losing his family farm to the wealthy. Even the city prophet corroborates this observation (see Isa. 5:8ff.).

When the prophet uses the word *covet*, he is reminding the reader of one of the fundamental commands of Israel's life: "thou shalt not covet," the tenth commandment in Exodus 20:17. The Hebrew word for covet is *chamad*, whose most fundamental meaning is to desire or to be passionate about. This meaning can be found in the activity of the people described. They think about only one thing from morning to night—acquiring more land: "Alas for those who devise wickedness and evil deeds on their beds! When the morning dawns, they perform it" (2:1). It is not that passion is wrong; it is wrong only when it's directed to the wrong object. Passion for God—"You shall love the Lord your God with all your heart, and with all your soul, and with all your might" (Deut. 6:5)—is central to the life of the Israelite. These thugs' desire for land and material gain preoccupies all of life and destroys the rural landscape.

What is most interesting about them? In the end what they most seek will be taken away from them—the land. After all, the land was God's gift to them in the first place. It does not belong to them by right. The fields they have taken away will be given away to the enemy, and these people will have no inheritance at all (2:4-5). Without the spiritual dimension to life, the landlords will lose the material things that had driven them most. As Christians we are reminded of Luke 12:13ff., where the rich fool thinks all of life is sustained by material things—and loses them all.

Discussion and Action

1. In this passage there is a turnaround, as those in Jerusalem are challenged to see themselves as responsible for the suffering of the abandoned cities. How do you

think they heard and understood this passage from the prophet Micah when it was first proclaimed to them? Consider dividing into smaller groups to devise role-plays illustrating possible responses to this prophecy.

2. It seems as if those in Jerusalem hope to survive at the expense of others, people who are their relatives and fellow-believers. How much is enough? How much is too much? When do we know that we have too much at the expense of others? How can we go about balancing the blessings of the world?

3. There is terrible suffering in different places in the world, some of which is preventable if proper help were given. If you looked at websites to find statistics about disparities between developed, developing, and undeveloped nations, share some of what you learned. What solutions, if any, do these websites suggest? As a group, pick one solution you can begin working on this very week. Set up a way of measuring success or failure in this endeavor.

4. In addition to considering what you might do, also discuss which leaders can and should be contributing to solving the problems of the world. Together work on composing a letter challenging leaders, and arrange for the letters to be sent.

5. The author talks about the way different regions around Jerusalem made fun of each other through the nicknames they used. What nicknames, preconceptions, prejudices, and other illusions are we ourselves guilty of when it comes to typing other people? What thoughtless attitudes have we projected through our attempts at humor? What meanness do we accept as a matter of course?

6. The author refers to the Thomas Ricks book, *Fiasco*, to talk about ways in which the behavior of some from the United States projects an image that is totally opposite of what we are used to thinking of ourselves. Could some of the accusations in this passage be used in reference to us? Why or why not? Are you comfortable with including observations about contemporary political situations in worship or Bible study? Why or why not?

7

A Ruler's Failed Response
Isaiah 7:1-17

Personal Preparation:

1. Read Isaiah 7:1-17. Highlight any verses that strike you as important or are familiar to you.
2. Read what a study Bible or commentary says about Isaiah 7:14 and Matthew 1:23. Take some notes, or bring the source with you to the group meeting.
3. Read Psalm 146. The psalm says "Do not put your trust in princes" and "Happy are those whose help is the God of Jacob." Make a short list of good and bad leaders, historical and current. Take time to pray for your national, state, provincial, and local leaders, whether you support them or not.
4. Provide a baby photo of yourself to the group leader, who will arrange them into a collage.

Suggestions for Sharing and Prayer

1. Greet one another with the words, "Today we share a sign of hope!" Invite the group to gather around the collage of baby pictures and try to identify each group member.
2. Play "Behold, a virgin shall conceive" and "O Thou that tellest good tidings to Zion" from Handel's *Messiah*. Read Isaiah 7:1-17 and Matthew 1:23 aloud. Discuss the political situation facing Isaiah and Ahaz. Why was it important for Isaiah to talk to the king? What was his basic message? Does that situation mirror our current situation today? To what extent is Isaiah's message one of hope? What provides hope in your life?
3. Put together a short dialogue that you imagine taking place between a present-day prophet and a present-day

leader that follows the lines of this passage. How would a present-day prophet word the message? How might it be received?

4. The session is titled "A Ruler's Failed Response." Talk about situations, small and large, where group members feel they failed in their response. What happened? How did people react? How easy was it to admit the failed decision?

5. Discuss the extent to which this group, or other groups of which you are a part, provide a place of trust where you can share failure as well as success, hope as well as correction. What elements are necessary to create such a setting?

6. Gather in a circle, sitting comfortably. Read (or play a recording of yourself reading) the guided meditation, "A Meeting Place with God," printed at the end of this session. As you close the meditation, invite group members to stretch.

7. Sing the hymn "To us a child of hope is born." Lead in a closing prayer of hope.

Understanding

Isaiah 7 is set in Jerusalem during preparations for war. God instructs Isaiah to look for the king, who is out inspecting the city's water resources. This stroll by the king was symptomatic of the high level of anxiety in the capital city. Isaiah's purpose is to comfort him with a message from the Lord.

Isaiah 7:1-2 depicts the formation of a coalition by Ephraim (the Northern Kingdom of Israel) and Syria in order to take the throne away from Ahaz, who was young—barely over twenty years old. They wanted Judah to join them in fighting the Assyrian king, Tiglath-pileser, because such an undertaking required the involvement of many nations. When Ahaz refused, they planned to depose him and elevate their choice for king, Tabe'el, which literally means "good for nothing." This would assure Judean support against the Assyrian king. When the Judeans heard of this, they "shook as trees . . . before the wind" (see also 2 Kgs. 16).

Isaiah reminds Ahaz that these two nations are nothing more than "smoldering firebrands" making a last ditch effort that will not succeed. When the prophet names these two leaders, he is reminding Ahaz that they are mere mortals. And he also reminds Ahaz that he is the head of the Judean state because God put him there by divine authority (2 Sam. 7:12ff.). Not only in this text, but also in Isaiah 31:1, the prophet declares that Judah remains under the authority and direction of God. So Ahaz should behave as one who has been divinely called, and not depend upon human strategies or upon horses and chariots.

The Call to Faith and Its Rejection

Given these circumstances, the prophet encourages the king to put away his fears. The prophet reminds the king that true protection lies with God. Brevard Childs observes: "Ahaz is challenged to ground his action upon God's promise to support him before his enemies. Undergirding the promise lies the divine covenant with the house of David (2 Sam. 7:12ff.), which had been directly threatened by the coalition (cf., v. 13). In a word, unless Judah, the people of God, understands itself as a theological reality—a creation of God and not a political entity—the state will have no future existence. King Ahaz, as the carrier of the Davidic promise, is called upon to respond for himself and his people to the reality of God's faithfulness" (64-65). This part of the passage ends with the call to "stand firm in faith." Political machinations will not secure the future for Judah, but faith will.

In verse 10, the prophet speaks to Ahaz a second time and encourages him to choose a sign from any region of the universe. But the king refuses the offer. On the surface, the king's response may be understood as pious, indicating that he trusts God enough to avoid relying on signs. But Isaiah discerns the king's true intent and his real political bent. The king has decided to trust Assyrian power rather than God's protection. (See 2 Kgs. 16:10ff., for a description of Ahaz's actions.)

At this response, the prophet explodes, telling the king that he has become a wearisome burden not only to his people, but also to God. In essence, the king has renounced the true authority of his throne and thereby relinquished his right to rule. How will God respond to this disobedience?

God's Promise in the Face of a Disobedient King

God answers the king through the prophet: "Look, the young woman is with child and shall bear a son, and shall name him Immanuel. He shall eat curds and honey . . . (7:14-15a). The Hebrew word *ha'almah* means "the young woman who is of marriageable age and fertile," as indicated by the fact that she is with child. The Hebrew text seems to imply that a specific woman will bear a child. This announcement of birth, name, and destiny appears elsewhere in the context of multiple wives to indicate legitimacy of the child who is to be born.

In the household of Abraham, Ishmael is the firstborn, but he is the son of Hagar. Sarah has been chosen to bear Abraham's heir and the same form of the oracle is repeated: "Your wife Sarah will bear you a son, and you shall name him Isaac. I will establish my covenant with him as an everlasting covenant . . . (Gen. 17:19). Isaac is chosen by divine intervention against the wishes of Abraham and the law of primogeniture. In the royal house of David, there were multiple wives, but only one queen mother. This oracle in Isaiah announces the continuity of the Davidic line by divine selection and promise.

The future king is not to be determined by the machinations of Ahaz, but by the eternal promises of God. The miracle of this text is that in the face of great Assyrian might and power, the throne of David will not be secured by bowing before Tiglath-pileser, but by the reliability of God's promise. This king is rejected, but the promise to the line of David is not.

As this text is translated many centuries later in the Septuagint, the Greek version of the Old Testament, the Hebrew word *'almah* is translated into the Greek as *parthenos*, meaning virgin. For this strand of tradition, the miracle is more than the continuity of David's line in the face of great danger, but includes the nature of the conception and birth of the new king. This one who was born of a virgin is carried forward into Matthew's Gospel (Matt.1:23).

Isaiah 7 and the Birth of Jesus

The context for the birth of Jesus is much like that in Isaiah. Jerusalem is under siege by the Romans. Later in the first century, the temple is destroyed and the people are scattered. It was easy to believe that God's promises had ended and the Davidic line would be forever destroyed. In this context the Gospel writer remembers the promise made in another dark period of Israel's life and announces the birth of the true Davidic heir. One level of the miracle lies in the fact that God stands behind centuries-old promises made. The second level of the miracle, maintained by the Greek tradition and centuries of church teaching, is the virgin birth. For me, the power of this passage is that God does not desert his people even when leaders disobey and make the wrong decisions. The meaning of the name of the Promised One is Immanuel, "God with us."

Though Isaiah, Ahaz, Pekah, and Rezin are long gone, this passage continues to have meaning today. Every year Christian believers celebrate the birth of Emmanuel. The birth itself reaches beyond any particular Advent season to the final coming of the Messiah. Yet in each Advent season we taste the presence of the one coming in the name of the Lord. We take comfort in the fact that we know the nature of his rule and the character of his realm. There is the temptation to side with Ahaz and settle for real politics, but we know better because we have seen the glory of the Lord in this Promised One.

Discussion and Action

1. When have you received good and bad advice? When have you given good and bad advice? What were the intentions of those giving the advice? How can you tell the difference between good and bad advice?
2. When it comes to friends and family, whom do you trust? Which political leaders do you trust? What are your criteria for determining trust and mistrust?
3. Based on what you know from the text and from other resource materials, describe the political situation facing Isaiah as he searches for King Ahaz. What are the choic-

es as Ahaz understands them? Why should Ahaz trust or distrust Isaiah?

4. The author talks about the meaning of the Hebrew word *'almah* as it relates to the Isaiah passage and to Matthew 1:23. Compare the meaning for Isaiah's time with what is generally the Christian interpretation of the verse. How important is interpretation when it comes to our understanding of scripture? Is it possible to have any understanding of a passage, sacred or secular, without some measure of interpretation? Explain.

5. What are we bequeathing to the next generation and the generation beyond because of political decisions made by our political leaders and by us? Identify good and bad outcomes of various decisions. How do you think our descendants will feel about what we are bequeathing to them?

6. How do you think Isaiah felt after the rejection of his message? Does faithfulness require success? Do our churches demonstrate faithfulness regardless of the possibility of success? Explain your responses.

7. Psalm 146 advises that we "not put [our] trust in princes." Make a short list of good and bad leaders, as you have experienced them in various arenas of life. Share a time of prayer for current national, state, provincial, and local leaders, whether or not you support them.

8. As a group, write and send letters of hope and encouragement to the children in your congregation.

A Meeting Place with God
A Guided Meditation

This meditation may be read aloud during the session, or recorded earlier to allow the leader to also enter into the experience. Take care not to rush through it. Allow space between sentences.

Close your eyes and relax. Take a deep breath. Picture a place where you are especially comfortable. This may be a spot in your home, or in a place where you have lived. It may not even exist anymore. But it is here now. It may be a place outdoors, far away, or close at hand. Find that spot. Picture yourself there.

Now, picture yourself rising and turning a corner, and in doing so, discovering that this place is even more perfect than you found it. It is a place now with an open door, an open space, where God can enter. You have come to a place where you know God is always present, always present for you. God is not rushed. God is not in a hurry to be elsewhere. God takes delight in who you are, and loves you for you. Walk into this special place and open your heart to God.

Don't worry about trying to see God or hear God. Simply be open to God. Let your special place expand as God is fully present with you. God is present with you now. God is always present with you, and God is always aware of you, but for the present you are fully aware of what is always the truth—God wants to meet with you.

Don't worry about greetings or acting in a special manner. Open your heart to be with God. If God has something special to say, God will say it to you. If God has a message, it will be delivered. Don't try to control the conversation. Be present with God, as God is always present in you. Don't hurry, don't try to direct.

The special place is always there, present just below the surface of the places we inhabit. God is inviting you to be present. Picture yourself seeing the people who share your life as God sees them. Examine each thing, each person, in your place, in your life, as God sees them.

Take time to breathe, to bless, and be blessed, to be in this special place where you become aware of what is always true—God is richly present in your life, in all lives.

Take a deep breath, and in your mind rise and turn a corner. Come back to this place where we are gathered. Bring your awareness of God with you, if you choose. Relax. You are still present with God; God is still present with you; and God is present with your sisters and brothers here in this place.

Open your eyes and stretch. Take a deep breath. Greet each other with smiles.

8

Announcement of a King and a New Style of Leadership
Isaiah 9:1-7; 11:1-9

Personal Preparation

1. Read Isaiah 9:1-7 and 11:1-9 aloud. These passages find a regular place in the observance of Christmas. What portions seem very familiar? What is unfamiliar?
2. Consult a commentary for historical background to the passages. Focus especially on meanings of the biblical word *righteousness*. Note the appearance of the word in both passages.
3. Look for artwork that illustrates the peaceable kingdom of Isaiah 11, or create your own. If possible, bring it with you to the session.
4. Check a reference work or the Internet for possible meanings for your name. How did you come to have this name? If there is time, do the same for others in your circle of family and friends.

Suggestions for Sharing and Prayer

1. Share what you learned about the meanings of your name. Which meanings seem most appropriate or accurate? Which seem least plausible?
2. Play "For behold, darkness shall cover the earth," "The people that walked in darkness," and "For unto us a Child is born" from Handel's *Messiah*. Then read Isaiah 9:1-7 and 11:1-9 aloud.

3. Christians often read into these passages the nativity of Jesus. How do the names in Isaiah 9 apply to your understanding of Jesus? What names do you give to Jesus?
4. The scripture is set at a low point in biblical history. Based on your reading, discuss the nature of the problem facing God's people. What parallels do you see to your own life or the life of your nation? What is the solution as proposed by Isaiah? What hope do you suppose this gave to people of that time? How do you interpret this message for our time?
5. The second Isaiah passage speaks to the healing of all of creation. Share some of the artwork you discovered that illustrates this passage. In what ways is nature broken in your area? What healing needs to take place? Arrange for the group to read the book or see the film *An Inconvenient Truth*.
6. These passages in Isaiah take place during a difficult time in the history of God's people. Describe a wilderness time in your own life, when you felt a lack of hope and great alienation. What place did God's Word or God's people have in bringing you to the place you are in today? What provided hope and help?
7. In your darkest hours, what gives you hope? Share insights. Close with prayer and sing the carol "Come, thou long-expected Jesus." There are some additional lyrics at the end of this session.

Understanding

Some people play Christmas music for only a few days, and some play it all year round. There are those who have a "Christmas Corner" in their homes, where sculptures of angels, shepherds, and mangers always have a place of honor. Today's passages from Isaiah are associated with Christmas. No matter the time of year, it's never a bad time to read them aloud.

In the previous session, we learned that Isaiah denounced King Ahaz because he rejected the guidance of God and chose an alliance with the king of Assyria, Tiglath-pileser. Ahaz chose this course of action because he feared he would be overthrown by the kings of Israel and Syria. He disregarded the advice of Isaiah, who told him that these two kings were worthless firebrands who would soon burn out. As a result, Isaiah turned his attention to the announcement of the birth of a new king who would embody the ideals and obedience expected of Davidic royalty.

In chapter 9, what Isaiah had predicted has already taken place. While Samaria, the capital city of the Northern Kingdom survived, much of the territory around the capital had been lost to the Assyrian conqueror. Three provinces had been created: the way of the sea; the land beyond the Jordan; and Galilee (9:1). The king of Israel had been defeated, and a whole series of rulers had followed one upon another in the north until the destruction of the capital city in 722 B.C.

Isaiah 9:4 looks to a future time when the darkness will be dispelled, as in the days when Gideon delivered the Israelites from the hand of Midian (Judg. 6–8). Neither the disobedient kings of Judah and Israel nor the king of Assyria will determine the future. There will come a time when those who walked in darkness will see a great light (Isa. 9:2).

What is this great light? It is the new king. Isaiah uses the familiar form of a birth announcement: "A child has been born for us, a son given to us" (9:6). Just as fathers used to await the announcement of birth in a hospital waiting room, so also in the Old Testament period the father awaited the news outside the delivery area in a designated location. In Isaiah 7, the focus was upon the mother and the continuity of the Davidic line. Isaiah 9 places the accent on the child who is to be the new ruler. However, the audience for this announcement is not a singular father or a family, but the household of faith, a people multiplied by the saving power of God (9:3).

A New Style of Leadership

Birth is followed by the choice of a name for the child. That's what happens in the second half of verse 6. Some of us have been involved in selecting the name for a child. Will the new child bear the name of a beloved family member, a friend, or will it be taken from a current hot list of names? I used to reflect on my name and whether or not I had lived up to it. I stopped thinking about that about forty years ago when I discovered that my middle name, Wilbur, means "wild boar" in Saxon. Sometimes naming seems to fit the child and at other times it does not. I really don't ask people about that in regard to my middle name!

Isaiah gives a list of names: "Wonderful Counselor, Mighty God, Everlasting Father, Prince of Peace." As one readily observes, these are not ordinary names. These titles are the names given to a royal heir. In Egypt, the pharaoh had five throne names, which were given at the time of his coronation and indicated the character of his rule—it was to be free of greed and corruption and filled with justice. The names used in Isaiah 9 are clearly meant to define the character of this new king. One name is not sufficient, and each one describes a different function of the divinely chosen king. How shall we understand these names? In Egypt, the names were designed to show that the pharaoh was a divine being. Such thinking is avoided in the Old Testament, where the king was seen instead as the adopted son of God (see Ps. 2:7).The only name that seems to alter this view is Mighty God. However, if *mighty* is translated "warrior," then *el* translated "God" might better be translated as "power" (see Gen. 31:29 and Mic. 2:1).

The true king then acts as a wise counselor who renders justice through special skills beyond ordinary vision (see 1 Kgs. 3 and Isa. 11:3b). The second name, Warrior of Power, describes characteristics normally associated with David, or it may be an oblique reference to Gideon (Judg. 6:12). The third title, Everlasting Father (or Father for the Age) suggests that the king provides protection for the widow and the orphan, the unprotected of society, the poor and the needy (Ps. 72; Isa.11:4). The fourth title (Prince of Peace) in Hebrew is *sar* and can be translated as "representative," "prince," "officer," or "trustee." The function then is to create peace and forms a fitting conclusion to this list. This leader, using the skills of counselor, warrior, and judge, is to bring peace. In the next verse, this outcome is accented by the phrase "his authority shall grow continually, and there shall be endless peace." This is the beginning of a messianic vision for the future, because God will establish this forevermore.

The Messianic Age

The vision begun in chapter 9 is now extended in Isaiah 11:1-9. The failure of the Davidic line is described in the metaphor of a stump. This royal line had failed in its responsibility, but God will raise a shoot from this family of Jesse. This cycle began with the miserable response of Ahaz and the heightened Assyrian threat. Against this backdrop the new leader will be blessed with the spirit that enhances all the characteristics described in chapter 9.

One additional characteristic is added to those outlined in Isaiah 9: "the fear of the Lord." This attribute is mentioned twice in the span of two verses. "In the Old Testament, the fear of Yahweh is, as it were, the summary of everything that can be said about the right attitude of man to God. . . . The king of the time of salvation will not presume upon his power, but know in his every act that he must give an account to God for every step he takes. He will be a wholly devout and righteous king, because God himself has given him his spirit" (Kaiser 158). Unlike Ahaz, this messianic king will be totally devoted to God and God's rule.

Just as in Isaiah 9, this passage ends with a declaration of peace, which is now extended to all creation: "The wolf shall live with the lamb, the leopard shall lie down with the kid" (11:6a). This is not a simple return to the beginning of time, but a new creation that has been prepared by God. Behaviors and activities will change. With the appropriate rule, all relationships are made new (see Isa. 65:25, which is set within the framework of the renewal of all creation). Appropriate rule brings healing to creation and all life. Actually, the declaration of the obedience of the Messiah in Mark's Gospel brings the healing of all creation: "And he was with the wild beasts; and the angels waited on him" (Mark 1:13b).

As Christians, we can readily understand why the Gospel writers depended on Isaiah for their description of the Messiah and the messianic age.

Discussion and Action

1. Name the animals you see in daily life. How do they fit together in the larger system of which you are a part? Compare the situation you observe with the description of the peaceable kingdom in Isaiah 11:1-9.
2. Name the best and worst qualities of the leaders around you. If they are no longer in power, how did they react when they were supplanted? How might they react to the word that a new king is born among them?
3. Read Revelation 22:1-7 aloud. These verses describe a tree whose leaves "are for the healing of the nations." How does this vision fit with Isaiah's description of the peaceable kingdom and the coming king?
4. The author gives an explanation for the names of the coming king. How were they important in Isaiah's time? How do some Christians relate these names to their understanding of Jesus?
5. A comedian once said that he believed the lion would lie down with the lamb, but he thought the lion would get a lot more sleep. How realistic do you find the vision of the peaceable kingdom for life as you live it?
6. Both passages suggest that the new ruler will judge "with righteousness." Where do you see righteousness occurring in the world today? What does real righteousness look like?
7. The author states that the fulfillment of this vision "is not a simple return to the beginning of time, but a new creation that has been prepared by God." What are the differences between the old and new creation, as you understand them? Have some aspects of the new creation become apparent in your world? What remains to be done? How much can be done by God alone?
8. One of the titles of the new king is Prince of Peace. Define peace as you understand it. How is it achieved, if at all? Is this something you have ever experienced? Does peace require a prince or ruler as an advocate? Explain.

Come, thou long-expected Jesus
Additional lyrics

The third stanza has an Advent/Christmas emphasis and may be eliminated if you choose.

Come God's people, be anointed, claim God's healing
    balm at last.
Set aside your pride and passion, Christ has fully paid the cost.
All that's fleeting, all that's passing, has its day,
    then fades away,
But your healing is forever, lasting past the final day.

Come God's people, claim God's pleasure, joys await to those
    who heed.
Nothing for the self-sufficient, everything to those in need.
Come now forward, and if limping, gladly lean so burdens
    bear,
Small and great, all harms are healing, if we have a tear
    to share.

Go, God's people, forth with treasure, not with gold or
    silver weighed.
With the lamp to light dark places, with the truth that can't be
    swayed.
From the manger comes the healer, who upon the cross
    in scorn
Bore our wounds and brought salvation, born to us on
    Christmas morn. [F. R.]

9

Little Bethlehem and the Least of the Houses of Judah
Micah 5:1-6

Personal Preparation

1. Read Micah 5:1-6 in different translations. What are the significant differences between translations? How do you account for these?
2. Look for songs about small towns or about a place you enjoy. Be prepared to play or sing this song.
3. Look for information on one of the following and bring to the group:
   - One of the most famous stories in Indiana basketball history concerns tiny Milan High School, which in 1954 defeated giant schools to take the state championship. This was fictionalized in the movie *Hoosiers*.
   - The work and ministry of Christian Peacemaker Teams.
   - The story behind the hymn "O little town of Bethlehem."
4. List the ways Bethlehem affected the history of God's people, according to the author of this study.

Suggestions for Sharing and Prayer

1. As you gather, sing "O little town of Bethlehem." Contemplate the state of things in your own place and in the Middle East. Offer sentence prayers for peace.
2. Even though it has a history with the family of David, Micah speaks about Bethlehem as an overlooked spot

from which a new king will emerge. Talk about an overlooked spot you enjoy. What is attractive about this spot?
Why do you think people overlook it? What are they
missing out on? If you were a prophet, how would you
proclaim the value of this place?

3. In Personal Preparation you were encouraged to research
a story. Share some of what you learned, and how these
lessons might apply to an interpretation of the present
passage.

4. The image of the king as shepherd throughout scripture
suggests that kings were intended to look out for the
welfare of the people rather than exert dominion. Micah
states that in response to the national insult of slapping
a king, God will raise up "seven shepherds" (v. 5). How
effective does that seem?

5. Read Micah 5:1-6 out loud. The passage begins with a terrible insult to the king. What is the worst insult that you
have endured? What was your response? Upon reflection,
how would you respond now? When have you insulted
another, intentionally or unintentionally? How did that
person respond? How, if ever, was the situation resolved?

6. Bethlehem means literally "house of bread." Share a loaf
of bread, breaking off pieces, as you play a recording of
"O little town of Bethlehem." Light a candle for peace,
and as the song plays, pray silently for peace for
Bethlehem and the world.

Understanding

I first saw Bethlehem when I was living in the southern outskirts
of Jerusalem in 1963. I lived on the edge of "no man's land,"
with barbed wire stretched on the other side of the street to guard
against trespassers. At night I could see the lights of the town in
the distance as I peered between the strands of barbed wire. In
my boyhood, I sang "O little town of Bethlehem" and had
images of peace and serenity. However, this birthplace of Judean
royalty was hardly a place of peace and serenity when Micah
preached, when Christ was born, or when I traveled to the
Middle East in 1963.

Micah 5:1-6 begins with an ominous description of a siege against Judah's chief city and the indignity suffered by the present king—a slap upon his cheek. Such action might indicate the cowering of someone like Hezekiah before Sennacherib in 701 B.C. The context is not unlike that of Isaiah 9:1, where the announcement of a new royal heir occurs at the time of great darkness: the Assyrian invasion and the division of the northern lands into provinces. Hope is born in these dire circumstances, much as it is expressed in my favorite Advent carol: "The hopes and fears of all the years are met in thee tonight." In these dire circumstances, the prophet proclaims God's continuing care for the people by calling a new leader.

Unlike Isaiah, who centers much of his thought in Jerusalem, Micah comes from the countryside. The emphasis for him is on Bethlehem of Ephrathah, a small town in Judah that is identified in the Book of Ruth as the home of Boaz, the forebear of Jesse, the father of David. This small town had no special status and is situated in one of the "little clans of Judah" (v. 2a). The emphasis falls on the smallness of the town and the low estate of the location.

Micah knew small towns could be overshadowed by the prestige of a large city like Jerusalem. He also knew that the vocabulary of humble origins could be overshadowed by the pomp and circumstance of the court. Thus, Micah returns to the origins of kingship, with its humble beginnings in the Judean countryside. He portrays the period before the monarchy moved into the large city and the qualities of a ruler that arise out of rural life.

Who Is the One Who Would Rule
The prophet takes his audience back to the earliest period "whose origin is from of old, from ancient days" (v. 2b). Such a reference brings to mind the selection of David as king. Samuel, the prophet, is directed to the house of Jesse to anoint the next king of Israel. Seven sons of Jesse pass before Samuel, but none of them are chosen. When Samuel suggests that Eliab, the oldest, should be chosen, God tells him, "Do not look on his appearance or on the height of his stature, because I have rejected him;

for the LORD does not see as mortals see; they look on the outward appearance, but the LORD looks on the heart" (1 Sam. 16:7). David is called in from tending the flocks, the lowest task of the household. When David appears, he is immediately chosen. Such an outlook on the boy is corroborated in the next chapter of 1 Samuel. Jesse tells David to take provisions to the battlefield where his brothers are stationed. When he arrives, Goliath taunts the Judean troops, who show their fear and run away. The young David shows no fear and offers to fight the Philistine. David's brothers then taunt him and ask him why he has left the sheep in the pasture. David persists because he knows that he does not face this giant alone, but God goes with him as a protective shield (1 Sam. 17:17ff.).

The enemy of God is defeated not by armament and horses, but by a small boy armed only with a slingshot. This is a far cry from future kings who shifted their loyalties from God to armies and alliances. To be sure, there is continuity in the Davidic line, but the relationship has more to do with simple beginnings without pretense of position or location of birth. Actually, the word *king* is not mentioned in this passage in Micah at all.

Service in the Name of the Lord

In Isaiah, the throne names and the specific task of the king are highlighted. In Micah, the emphasis falls on the origin of the rule: 1) "from you shall come forth for me" (v. 2); 2) "feed his flock in the strength of the Lord" (v. 4); and 3) "in the majesty of the name of the Lord his God" (v. 4). These definitions of the new ruler highlight the lordship of Israel's God, into whose service the true leader is called. The emphasis is not on the specific skills of the ruler, but on ultimate dependence on God's guidance and direction.

I am reminded of the text in Judges where Gideon is asked to be king. He responds, "I will not rule over you, and my son will not rule over you; the LORD will rule over you" (Judg. 8:23). Gideon recognizes that his leadership has been God-directed and God-given. Rule depends upon seeing the lordship of God over all of history. Micah highlights this particular dimension of early Israelite tradition—a time of simplicity before the monarchy became entrenched and dependent on military strength and alliances.

By depending on God, the people are cared for as a shepherd tends his flock by providing security and food. The scattered flock is brought together again: "the rest of his kindred shall return to the people of Israel" (v. 3b). At the front of the Pittsburgh Church of the Brethren building (where I was baptized) was a large stained glass window with Jesus as the Good Shepherd, cradling a lamb. I always saw myself as the lamb cradled in the Shepherd's arm. Below the window were the words, "Come unto me all ye who labor and are heavy laden, and I will give you rest." The true leader brings rest to the people of God and provides a sense of security through their confidence in the presence of the one true Lord.

This leadership of which Micah speaks brings about peace (v. 5a). As I was completing this lesson, I listened to an interview with John Danforth, former senator from Missouri and an Episcopal priest. He claimed that the religious task in our time and in all times is one of reconciliation. Religious commitment, he said, should bring about peace. Both Micah and Isaiah agree on this; the new ruler, as the true shepherd, will be an instrument of peace. Every Advent, some of the most powerful words recited are those from Micah repeated in Matthew 2:6: "And you, Bethlehem, in the land of Judah, by no means least among the rulers of Judah; for from you shall come a ruler who is to shepherd my people Israel."

Bethlehem is still a small town caught up in a larger web of conflict. People stream there to celebrate the Prince of Peace— when they are allowed to. As in 1963 when I was on that hillside far away in Jerusalem, but with Bethlehem in full view, sojourners and pilgrims alike can still hear the faint strains of my favorite Advent hymn, "The hopes and fears of all the years are met in thee tonight."

Discussion and Action

1. Compare the historical context, as revealed in this study and in commentaries or study Bibles you may have

consulted, with a New Testament interpretation that sees this passage as also applying to the history of Jesus.

2. Micah refers to Bethlehem as if he assumes that the big-city people of Jerusalem have forgotten the place this small city played in the history of God's people. In your opinion, what small towns have made an obvious, but obviously overlooked, contribution to the world? What do you think causes some people to overlook small towns that have played a big part in history?

3. The passage speaks of a great insult to the king that has to be endured. When nations are insulted, how do they usually respond? What alternatives are there to violence? What creative ways can be followed or found to prevent wars, rather than plant the seeds for new ones?

4. Reflect on the history of Bethlehem as described by the author. What lessons might contemporary rulers in the Middle East take from this passage and this history, as well as from the story of Jesus?

5. Working in smaller groups or individually, rewrite Micah 5:1-6 in your own words to respond to a current situation in the Middle East or another hotspot around the world.

6. The author quotes former senator John Danforth, who said "that the religious task in our time and in all times is one of reconciliation." In your experience, do religious leaders generally work toward reconciliation, or do they fan the flames of violence? Share examples to back up your response. What have you or your church done to advance the cause of reconciliation, both close at hand and in the world at large?

7. Do you experience "shepherd leadership" in your congregation? in your life? What should such leadership look like? How would it operate? Offer some stories from your experience. What might your congregation do to model servant leadership if faced with insults from your community and the world?

10

A Shared Hope for the Future
Isaiah 2:1-5; Micah 4:1-5

Personal Preparation

1. Read Isaiah 2:1-5 and Micah 4:1-5 aloud. Lay the texts side by side, so you can compare them verse by verse. Highlight verses that are basically the same and also those that differ.
2. Isaiah was a city prophet and Micah was a country prophet. Which of the differences in these texts could grow out of these perspectives?
3. Write a paragraph or draw a picture of your concept of a perfect place. What elements of the city would be present? What elements of the country would be present?
4. Pick one of these passages and consider what each verse has to say. Pray for the fulfillment of that verse in God's time. Pray for leaders and for people you know, that they might receive the benefits of the passage.

Suggestions for Sharing and Prayer

1. Open by singing "Come, we that love the Lord." Between stanzas, read the passages from Isaiah and Micah. Invite one-sentence statements about God's plan for history.
2. Continue by playing the "Hallelujah Chorus" from Handel's *Messiah*. Invite words of praise for God and for God's good works. Set out a long sheet of newsprint, and sketch all of creation being drawn to Mount Zion. What can you bring to help make the world whole?
3. Both passages point to a time of comfort and security for all people. What is necessary for people around the

world to experience comfort and security? What might you be willing to give up so that others can share in a measure of prosperity?

4. Dramatize a dialogue between Isaiah and Micah. Imagine that they are walking together uphill toward Mount Zion. What do they say to each other? On what do they agree? Are there things they disagree about? What advice can they give each other about the city and the country?

5. Turn to the paragraph that begins, "Some years ago I listened to a German scholar talk about the resurrection." Discuss your reactions to that paragraph and the light that guides your own path.

6. Read aloud Psalm 121; then sing "Great is thy faithfulness." Pray portions of Isaiah 2:1-5 and Micah 4:1-5, selecting verses and incorporating them into prayers for all people.

7. Some have said that history begins with a garden in Genesis and ends with a city in Revelation. In Revelation 21 and 22, the description of the New Jerusalem includes substantial vegetation and garden space. What would the perfect combination of city and country look like?

8. Close by playing "Worthy is the Lamb" from Handel's *Messiah*. As you listen, remember both the harsh words and the words of hope spoken by Isaiah and Micah, and reflect on their vision of God's goal for all of God's people.

Understanding

As a young boy, I can remember singing with gusto "We're marching to Zion, beautiful, beautiful Zion, that beautiful city of God." At that stage of my life, I drew great comfort from this hymn. My parents had separated; we lost our first home; I lived with an uncle and aunt; my mother was looking for a new home for our family. My family's life was in turmoil because we lacked a resting place. The song offered a permanence I lacked in my everyday life. It was a comfort to know that there was somewhere that the journey would end and where peace would prevail.

Both of this session's passages offer the comfort of knowing where our journey ends and where peace will prevail. However, though these prophetic books contain a common vision for the future, the interpretations are different. While there are slight variations in text between Micah and Isaiah, it appears that the prophets shared a common oracle about the city of God and its role in the future relations of the nations. We will look at this common vision before we look at the different interpretations in the two books.

A Common Vision
For both Isaiah, the city prophet, and Micah, the country seer, this journey would include a walk uphill toward Mount Zion both literally and symbolically. But even though they are going to the same place, they—and other biblical writers—see the journey differently. In the Psalter there is a series of "Songs of Ascent" (Ps. 120–134). While the meaning of the title is debated, scholars agree that these songs were sung by pilgrims on their way to Jerusalem, to Zion, where the temple of God was located.

Psalm 122 begins with the words "Let us go to the house of the Lord!" The Psalm goes on to say: "To it the tribes go up, the tribes of the LORD, as was decreed for Israel, to give thanks to the name of the LORD. For there the thrones for judgment were set up, the thrones of the house of David. Pray for the peace of Jerusalem: 'May they prosper who love you. Peace be within your walls, and security within your towers' " (Ps. 122:4-7). When people are uprooted and under attack, "home" provides an orientation and a bearing for the facing of life. Jerusalem offered that center for the Israelite people.

The common vision of Isaiah and Micah extends beyond the house of Israel and now includes many people who, like the Israelite pilgrims of Psalm 122, cry out: "Come, let us go to the mountain of the LORD, to the house of the God of Jacob" (Isa. 2:3a and Mic. 4:2a). These nations and peoples want to be taught with the instruction and the Word of the Lord that can be found in Jerusalem. Their search is for right understanding and knowledge. The nations seem to have lost their way in terms of states-manship and relationships with one another. In this instance the instruction comes directly from God, since the rulers of this world have lost their way and can no longer be relied upon for sound judgment and correct direction.

An encounter with the living Lord changes the way in which the nations interact with one another. In this vision they become aware of the larger purposes of God, a vision that reverses the call to war into a call to peace. Implements of war are turned into plowshares and pruning hooks. As nations come to consider the ways of God, they discover the pathways of peace. It should not be surprising that these words are written on the halls of the United Nations. In an age of terror, this vision suggests that path-ways toward peace should direct all our thoughts as a people of faith and encourage us to witness to the alternatives to war.

Isaiah's Interpretation in 2:5

Isaiah concludes the vision with the advice, "O house of Jacob, come, let us walk in the light of the LORD!" What is this light? In my view it is the vision that the prophet has just propounded. This oracle precedes all the words of judgment we have reviewed in this study where both the king and his people are found with their eyes shut to the power of God. This vision is also for us and for all those who followed the aftermath of the destructive power of Assyria on Judah and Jerusalem. This oracle stands at the beginning, so that the redemptive purpose of God lies behind all that is to follow.

Some years ago I listened to a German scholar talk about the resurrection. He said it is like a great light that informs the pil-grimage of every Christian. If we try to look into it, we will be blinded because we cannot penetrate it. However, if we allow it to light our way, then we will be able to walk in the only light that matters, even in the most difficult of times. This oracle, like the resurrection, shows the redemptive purpose of God that is not diminished in times of upheaval and dislocation. To walk in such light preserves the pilgrim when the way seems unclear.

Micah's Interpretation in 4:4-5

Micah extends the vision that is shared with Isaiah. He further universalizes it by referring to "nations far away" (v. 3a). In addition, he describes the outcome of this drive toward peace: "they shall all sit under their own vines and . . . fig trees" (v. 4a). The economic burden of militarism is removed and agrarian independence emerges. The cost of the monarchy, which was built for protection and security, is no longer necessary. Energies may now be directed to economic development and the long-term well-being of communities. It takes time to grow vineyards and orchards, yet in this new environment no one is afraid to build. "And no one shall make them afraid" (v. 4).

Micah concludes the vision with the words, "The mouth of the LORD of hosts has spoken." He turns to interpretation in verse 5. Micah notes that peoples of the world will still walk in the name of their gods. The transformation has not been completed. After all, this oracle follows the predicted devastation of Jerusalem in Micah 3:9-12. The proclamation is for the future role of this place. For the believer, Micah writes, "We will walk in the name of the LORD our God forever and ever (v. 5b). Micah calls the community of faith to live in this profound vision of peace even before the world is transformed.

Conclusion

Isaiah used the oracle as way to view the judgment of Judah and Jerusalem. Micah presents it as a way to think and behave after judgment has occurred and before the renewal of the universe has been completed. In the end, both city prophet and country seer, in addressing the specific problems of their shared era, looked beyond their time to the timeless significance of their faith and action. In this way they insured that both the city dwellers and the country folks in every age would address contemporary problems with a faith in God's desire for peace and its establishment in a world broken apart by war.

Discussion and Action

1. What are the differences and similarities of the two passages from Isaiah and Micah? What is each prophet saying? How significant are the differences?

2. What is needed for all people to have the security of sitting under their own vines and under their own fig trees? What corresponds to a vine and fig tree for you?

3. Reflect on the words, "they shall beat their swords into plowshares, and their spears into pruning hooks; nation shall not lift up sword against nation, neither shall they learn war any more." Is this a realistic hope? What examples come to mind of ways in which swords have been beaten into plowshares? On the other hand, what plowshares have been converted into swords? What role does technology play regarding things that make for peace and things that make for war? Is it possible for nations to convert to ways of peace, or must one always be ready for war? Explain your response.

4. Isaiah and Micah have been pictured throughout this study as city and country prophets. Which prophet has spoken more to your needs or reflected your understanding of the world? Why and in what way?

5. On occasion some of these sessions have invited us to take a scholar's view in the interpretation of what are most likely well-known passages (e.g., by explaining the meaning of Hebrew words). What is the place for this kind of learning in our interpretation? Has your understanding been strengthened by these insights?

6. Reflect on all ten sessions. Which sessions spoke most forcefully to you and why? Which passages seem most important to you? Why? In general, do you find study of the Old Testament easy or difficult? Do you prefer to study the Old Testament, the New Testament, or a balance? Sum up what you have learned from the ten sessions of this study. What were the surprising things? What do you feel you have always known?

Bibliography

Albright, William Foxwell. *From Stone Age to Christianity.* Baltimore: Johns Hopkins Press, 1940.

Buber, Martin. *The Prophetic Faith.* New York: Harper and Brothers, 1949.

Childs, Brevard S. *Isaiah* (Old Testament Library). Louisville: Westminster John Knox Press, 2001.

Hillers, Delbert R. *Micah.* Philadelphia: Fortress Press, 1984.

Kaiser, Otto. *Isaiah 1-12.* Philadelphia: The Westminster Press, 1972.

Limburg, James. *Hosea-Micah* (Interpretation Series). Atlanta: John Knox Press, 1988.

Pritchard, James Bennett, ed. *Ancient Near Eastern Texts Relating to the Old Testament.* Princeton, N.J.: Princeton University Press, 1969.

Ricks, Thomas E. *Fiasco: The American Military Adventure in Iraq.* New York: The Penguin Press, 2006.

Wolff, Hans Walter. *Micah: A Commentary* (Augsburg Continental Commentary Series). Minneapolis: Augsburg Fortress Publishers, 1990.

Other Covenant Bible Studies

Each book is $6.95 plus shipping and handling. For a full description of each title, ask for a free catalog of these and other Brethren Press titles. Major credit cards accepted. Prices subject to change.

Regular Customer Service hours are Monday through Friday, 8:30 a.m. to 5:30 p.m. CT.

Brethren Press • 1451 Dundee Avenue • Elgin, Illinois 60120
Phone: 800-441-3712 • Fax: 800-667-8188
e-mail: brethrenpress_gb@brethren.org
www.brethrenpress.com